Managing Risk of Financial Models

A Smart and Simple Guide for the Practitioner

Aruna Joshi, Ph.D., FRM

Copyright © Aruna Joshi 2017

All rights reserved in all media. No part of this publication may be used or reproduced without prior written permission, except for brief quotations embodied in critical articles and reviews. Any person who does any unauthorized act in relation to this publication may be liable to criminal prosecution and civil claims for damages.

Published in USA

Cover Design: Meera Joshi

Editors: Arun Majumdar and Shalini Majumdar

This book is dedicated to my husband, Arun Majumdar whose encouragement and nagging made this book possible and my parents Avinash and Mandakini Joshi who have been my constant support through life's ups and downs.

Just when I think I have learned the way to live,
life changes.

~ by Hugh Prather

Table of Contents

Chapter 1: Who Needs Model Risk Management 1

Chapter 2: Introduction to Model Risk 4

Chapter 3: Model Identification 11

Chapter 4: Model Inventory 16

Chapter 5: Model Risk Rating... 23

Chapter 6: Model Validation 34

Chapter 7: Findings and Recommendations......................... 49

Chapter 8: Templates for Documentation and Validation 56

Chapter 9: Model Monitoring... 63

Chapter 10: Model Risk Reporting.. 67

Chapter 11: Hypothetical Case Study................................... 73

Chapter 1: Who Needs Model Risk Management

"When models turn on, brains turn off."
~ Til Schuermann

The word "model" may evoke ideas of curves and gossamer skin you see in fashion magazines. This book, however, deals with models in banking terms which could not be more different. In banking, the word "model" is used in the context of simulating situations encountered during day to day operations. For instance, have you ever wondered why two borrowers with similar FICO® scores are quoted very different mortgage rates by the same bank? Or why some banks remained solvent with their reputations intact while others failed during the Great Recession[1] of 2008? Why red flags are raised when some customers wire $10,000 or more but not for other customers?

I joined the financial services industry more than a decade ago as a **quant**[2] in the Risk Management department, who learned that answers to such questions are often determined by using mathematical and statistical techniques called "models". Models are

---

[1] The Great Recession is a term that represents the sharp decline in economic activity during the late 2000s, which is generally considered the largest downturn since the Great Depression.
[2] an expert at analyzing and managing quantitative data

used through a process **called Model Risk Management** which is effectively a formalized process to identify, assess and mitigate financial risk arising from use of these models. After I peered through several policies and procedures and published literature (basically learning on the job), I discovered the need for an easy-to-follow basics for newcomers into Model Risk Management. My Masters in Financial Engineering prepared me for Market Risk, Credit Risk, Derivatives Valuation etc. however did not prepare me for this!

Even if you're not in the banking industry, but are curious as to how banks use models, if you are a statistician or mathematically inclined or are interested in risk management, look no further. I have simplified the process in an easy-to-read format so even a novice can understand it. You will get a feel for the intricate process refined over the years by model risk practitioners. You will learn what the bank regulators are looking for in a solid model risk management program.

This book describes, at a high level, all aspects required for developing and maintaining a strong model risk management program at any institution from a practitioner's view. You will learn about: model identification, creating a model inventory, risk rating of models that determine the rigor and frequency of model review, aspects of model reviews also known as model validation, management of model review recommendations that arise from model reviews, and model risk reporting so senior management is aware of model risk within the financial institution.

The last chapter walks the reader through a hypothetical example showing how all aspects of model risk management come together to bring the process to life.

Chapter 2: Introduction to Model Risk

"Essentially, all models are wrong, but some are useful."~ George E.P. Box

Models are essentially simplified versions of reality to analyze real world situations. An engineer may use a computer model of a building to test whether it can withstand severe earthquakes, where as a biologist may make a physical model of DNA to understand its chemical properties better. In the finance and insurance industry, models are used to make business decisions such as whether a financial institution has enough reserves to cover losses, or the likelihood that a certain borrower will default on a loan so the loan can be priced appropriately.

In the past decade, banking, insurance, and investment management firms have seen proliferation of novel financial instruments. These instruments are so complex that it is difficult to predict their performance in an ad hoc manner; they require sophisticated financial models to do so. Advances in quantitative techniques, computing power and software applications have contributed greatly to the reliance on such models to make business decisions. Scores of new models had to be created and introduced to meet regulatory requirements to ensure that banks have enough capital through stress testing (e.g. as mandated by Federal Reserve Board's CCAR - **Comprehensive Capital Analysis and Review**[3]).

The use of models involves risks. Even though the model may be correct, sometimes the input data may be inaccurate, making its predictions misleading. Sometimes predictions may be correct, but there are inherent uncertainties, which make the business decisions difficult. And there are times when the model itself is faulty. Without an understanding of these risks, it is difficult to make judicious decisions about their use. Therefore, management of model risk, especially in the financial services industry, has gained immense importance.

Let us get more precise about the definition of a model and its risks.

A "**model**," as defined in the FRB (Federal Reserve Board) SR 11-7 (2011)[4] supervisory guidance on model risk management, is a quantitative method, system, or approach that applies statistical, economic, financial, or mathematical theories, techniques, and assumptions to process input data into quantitative estimates.

Models are simplified representations of real-world relationships among observed characteristics, values, and events. *The risk of such simplifications leading to an*

---

[3] Comprehensive Capital Analysis and Review (CCAR) is a United States regulatory framework introduced by the Federal Reserve in order to assess, regulate, and supervise large banks and financial institutions.

[4] This regulatory guidance provides banks with a comprehensive framework for deploying an enterprise-wide model risk management program. Examiners now expect banks to use such a framework when designing, implementing and improving all models.

*inaccurate representation of reality is referred to as **model risk.***

More specifically, model risk for a financial institution is defined as the possibility of incurring a financial loss, making incorrect business decisions, misstating external financial disclosures, or damaging the institution's reputation. This risk arises from:

– Errors in the model design and development process — such as errors in the data, theory, statistical analysis, assumptions, or computer code underlying a model, or in the model developer's judgment

– Errors that occur as the model is implemented and deployed into a production environment

– Errors in model operation once in production

– Misapplication of models, or model results, by users

– Use of models whose performance has deteriorated over time from its original development

Let us consider a couple of case studies.

Case Study #1

In 1998 the hedge fund LTCM (Long-Term Capital Management) in 1998 collapsed resulting in a $1.85 billion in loss. LTCM's core investment strategy was loosely based on **arbitrage**, the simultaneous purchase and sale of an financial asset to profit from a difference in the price. In arbitrage, the asset does not change (e.g. shares of Apple, Inc.). LTCM's strategy was based on *convergence trading* which is similar to arbitrage, however here the assets are not identical but similar (e.g. shares of Apple, Inc. vs. shares of Amazon, Inc.: since both these companies are in technological sector they are expected to behave similarly) LTCM used quantitative models to execute their strategy. Because the magnitude of discrepancies in valuations in this kind of trade is small, LTCM used high **leverage** and **hedged** against a predictable range of **volatility** (rapid change and uncertainty) in foreign currencies and bonds. One of the currencies used was the Russian ruble. When Russia declared it was devaluing its currency, it defaulted on its bonds. That event was beyond the normal range that LTCM had estimated using their models that favored high leverage. Not surprisingly, the fund collapsed.

Case Study #2:

> Another example is that of JP Morgan's $6 billion trading loss in 2012, also referred to as *London Whale*. One London-based quantitative analyst was working on a new VaR (Value at Risk) model in MS Excel®. **Value at Risk** means how much a set of investments might lose, given normal market conditions, in a set time period such as a day or week etc.. During investigation, it was found that not only was the model tested incorrectly, it also suffered from standard Excel flaws. For example, the model operated through a series of Excel spreadsheets, which had to be completed manually, by a process of copying and pasting data from one spreadsheet to another. There also appears to have been a faulty equation in the model. **Volatility** appeared lower than it was because of issues with this model. The model seriously underestimated the downside of its synthetic credit portfolio and the bank had to declare a loss of $6 billion.

The above case studies underscore the importance of managing model risk. The formal discipline of managing model risk is also becoming more mature. In the original guidance, namely OCC 2000-16 (2000) issued by the Office of the Comptroller of the Currency, Model Risk Management mainly focused on the narrow area of independent model validation or a thorough review of the model. The focus has shifted to a broader risk management approach over the last few years spurred by the newer OCC 2011-12 (2011) and FRB SR 11-7 (2011) model risk management guidance.

See Figure 2.1 below for the evolution of model risk management.

Key Takeaways

- Models are simplified representations of real-world relationships among observed characteristics, values, and events. *The risk of such simplifications leading to an inaccurate representation of reality is referred to as **model risk**.*
- Financial Institutions such as banks are expected to comply with regulatory guidance from Federal Reserve Board - **SR 11-7** to manage their model risk
- Key aspects of effective model risk management include model development, implementation, use, validation, and governance

FIGURE 2.1. Evolution of Model Risk Management in Banking (source: *MODEL RISK AND THE GREAT FINANCIAL CRISIS: THE RISE OF MODERN MODEL RISK MANAGEMENT* Jeffrey A. Brown, Brad McGourty, Til Schuermann, Oliver Wyman, 7 January 2015)

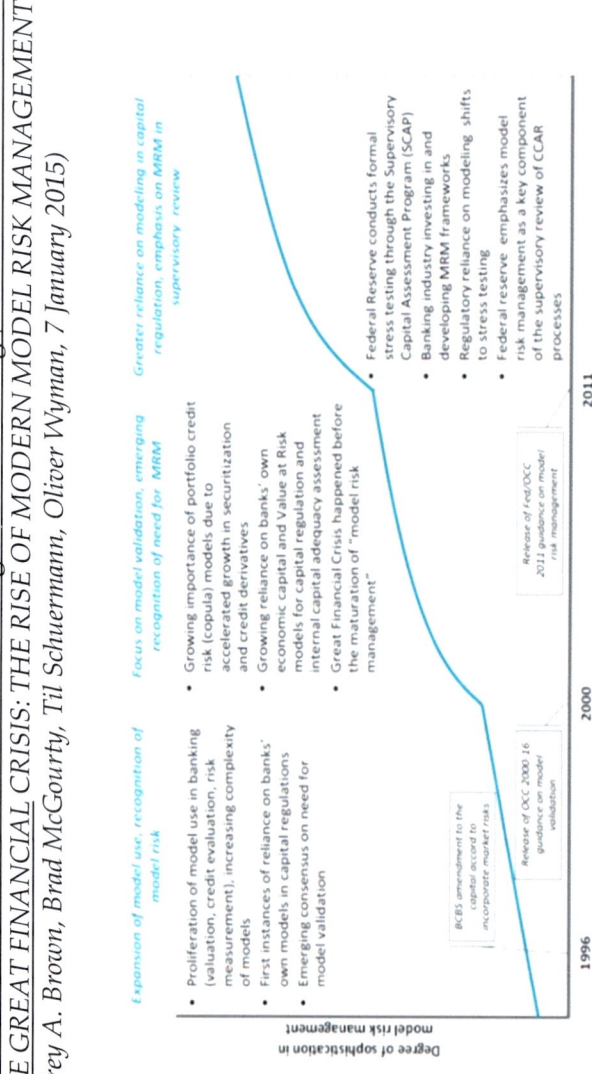

Chapter 3: Model Identification

"Be sure you positively identify your target before you pull the trigger" ~ Tom Flynn

What is a model?

Now that we know we are not talking about the curves and gossamer skin when we discuss models, to determine if a quantitative process is categorized as a model, banking institutions typically have a formalized process. In FRB's SR 11-7 (model risk management guidance as described in Chapter 2), a model is defined as a process that consists of three components:

- an information input component, which delivers assumptions and data to the model;
- a processing component, which transforms inputs into estimates;
- and a reporting component, which translates the estimates into useful business information

If the quantitative process meets all the components, the process is deemed to be a model. Some institutions make the process a little more granular. They may have several questions that are applied to determine the nature of the process. Examples include:

- Is the process a simplified representation of real-world relationships among observed characteristics, values, and events?

- Is considerable subjective judgment exercised at various stages of development, implementation, use, or validation?
- Does the process take an input related to assumptions or data to the "process"?
- Does the process transform inputs into estimates using a quantitative technique?
- Does the process produce quantitative estimates of uncertain values? (not definitive outputs based on fixed or prescribed calculations)

Typically, if the answer to all these questions is yes, the process is categorized as a model.

Models need governance, or oversight, to ensure all stakeholders are involved and informed. For effective model risk management, according to SR 11-7 guidance, all models need to be validated, their performance be monitored routinely and a periodic review of all models needs to be conducted in the cycle when they are not being validated. For effective model governance, all models in a financial institution should be part of a repository or a centralized database where all model related activities can be recorded. This is discussed in Chapter 4.

Where do models reside in banks?

Banks have several lines of business such as retail banking (for consumers), commercial banking (for corporate clients), treasury, operational risk, and finance. Most of these lines of business use certain quantitative process to make business decisions. For example, retail banking may use proprietary credit underwriting **scorecards**[5] to qualify borrowers for loans where as treasury may use quantitative processes for asset liability management. That explains why someone may not qualify for the home loan when they had a ballooning credit with six different credit cards! The compliance department uses models to score borrowers based on their risk of money laundering, whereas finance uses models to estimate expenses as required for stress testing.

Determining if a particular quantitative process is a model is as much an art as science. In most instances, there is no ambiguity. Consider estimating the probability of whether a homeowner will default on a mortgage loan. The estimate will require statistical techniques and depend on variables like borrower's FICO® score, loan to value, loan type etc. That is clearly a model since it relies on assumptions as to which risk drivers are important. This is fundamentally different from using an Excel spreadsheet that takes several cash flows in as input and calculates the net present value or internal rate of return: the excel method is not a model since there is no ambiguity on the final result. The formulas are based on definitions and hence it can be categorized as a calculator, not a model.

Questions arise in instances that are a bit more ambiguous. An example is when estimates are made using a qualitative approach such as assuming that a

---

[5] These scorecards are similar to FICO® scores. FICO score is a score specific to a borrower based on the person's credit history where as the credit underwriting scorecard usually takes the borrower aspects as well as loan aspects such as loan-to-value, loan amount etc.

particular outcome is dependent on a **macroeconomic factor**[6] with no statistical support. In other words, the relationship is not determined by any regression, trendline, etc. For example, an organization may assume a straight line forecast to project revenues where revenues grow linearly with GDP (Gross Domestic Product). Such a process can be categorized as either an assumption or a model. However, in order to have good governance over such processes, more and more are being categorized as models by institutions since the process is still defined as a mathematical relationship *albeit* very elementary.

---

[6] Macroeconomic factors are events or situations that affect the economy on a broader level, influencing the economic outcome of large groups of people on a national or regional level. Some macroeconomic factors include unemployment, savings, inflation and investments.

Key Takeaways

- Models reside in several lines of business in a bank such as retail banking, commercial banking, treasury etc.
- Determining if a particular quantitative process is a model is an art as much as science
- Model risk management departments have formalized processes to determine if a quantitative process is a model that needs to follow SR 11-7 guidelines

Chapter 4: Model Inventory

"If you count all your assets you always show a profit." ~ Wilson Mizner

Creating and maintaining an inventory for all models that the bank uses benefits a bank of any size or complexity. What should a model inventory contain? To design an inventory that is comprehensive, consider the model lifecycle as shown in Figure 4.1 below. Once the model is developed, regulatory guidance mandates that the model needs to be validated before it is implemented. Finally, as a new version of the model is developed, the old version is retired. Model inventory should capture as many aspects of the model cycle as possible.

FIGURE 4.1. Model Lifecycle Schematic

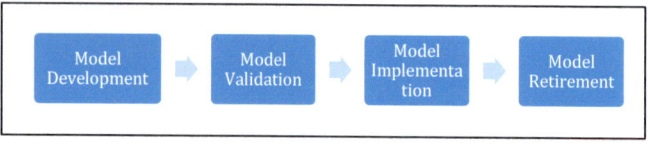

At a high level, for each model, this inventory should include the model's general information (ID, version etc.), model development information such as purpose, business line responsible for the model, person responsible for the model (also referred to as model owner), model inputs and outputs, etc.

As mentioned earlier, SR 11-7 also mandates a review of models (model validation) by an independent group within the bank. Additionally, since some models have a larger impact than others, models are typically categorized or rated in terms of risk they pose to the institution. This topic is discussed in detail in Chapter 5. Hence, information such as the risk rating of the model and the status of the model's validation should also be saved in the inventory. Model implementation aspects such as the date it went into use and approved uses should also be saved.

Since some models are discontinued due to either performance degradation or new versions being developed, information for when a model is discontinued should also be a part of the inventory. In addition, major issues/findings identified during validation review or internal audit review should also be tracked in the inventory and discussed in a later section. This topic is discussed in Chapter 7.

Periodic management attestation to the accuracy and completeness of the model inventory should also be conducted to help ensure that the inventory is appropriately maintained. Periodic review (at least annual) of the model even after it has been validated is also specified in the SR 11-7 guidance, hence dates to determine the next review cycle should also be recorded.

An accurate and complete model inventory is not the responsibility of the Model Risk Management team alone but that of the entire organization. The Model Risk Management department is usually responsible for the logistics of maintenance with input from all stakeholders.

Table 4.1 shows suggested field names that are typically included in the model inventory. This list is not comprehensive but merely suggests elements that are considered best practices. Fields can be added or removed as appropriate.

TABLE 4.1 Suggested Model Inventory Fields

Group	Field Name	Comments
General Model Information	Model ID	
	Model Version	
	Model Name	
	Model Status	In use, in development or discontinued etc.
Stage I: Model Development	Date Added to the Inventory	
	Application Environment	SAS, Excel
	Development: Internal/External	Internal or vendor or developed using external sources
	Model Type	Statistical, Conceptual
	Model Owner Name	
	Model Owner Group	Line of Business
	Model Purpose/Product(s)	CCAR, Origination etc.
	Model Developer Name	
	Model Development Group	

Managing Risk of Financial Models • 19

	Model Development Completion Date	
	Type of Model's Inputs	Whether inputs are macroeconomic variables or other models
	Source of Model's Inputs	Inputs sourced from external or internal sources
	Model Outputs	
Stage II: Model Validation	**Model Risk Rating**	High, Medium, Low etc.
	Model Validator	
	Validation: Internal/External	
	Date of Last Validation	
	Date of Next Expected Validation	
	Date of Last Annual Review	
	Date of Next Expected Annual Review	
	Model Validation Status	Approved, declined etc.
	Approval Conditions	
	Model Use Limitations	CCAR (Comprehensive Capital Analysis and Review) or BAU (Business as Usual)
	Data Limitations	
	Exceptions to Policy	
Stage III: Model Implementation	**Date Model Implemented**	
Stage IV: In Use	**Date Model Went "In Use"**	
	Approved Model Use(s)	CCAR, BAU
	Model User (Contact Person)	

	Model User Group	
	Date of Last Annual Review	
Stage V: Discontinued	Date Discontinued	
	Reason Discontinued	
	Attachments: Reason Discontinued	
Attestation	Attestation: Model Owner	
	Attestation: Manager Level Approval	
	Attestation: Date	

Let us go back to the example of a custom-built credit underwriting scorecard that a bank may use to qualify borrowers for an automobile loans developed in SAS. In the Model Development section of the inventory, the data entered for the model would be according to Table 4.2.

The type of data to be entered in other sections is self-explanatory.

Model inventory is maintained by the model governance team within the Model Risk Management Department with secure access to stakeholders such as model validators, model owners, risk managers within each line of business etc. Model inventory is also shared with regulators during regulatory examinations, hence it is imperative that the model inventory is as comprehensive and accurate as possible.

TABLE 4.2 Suggested Model Inventory Fields

Development	Internal
Model Type	Statistical, Conceptual
Model Owner Group	Retail Banking Group
Model Purpose/Product(s)	Origination
Type of Model's Inputs	Loan attributes e.g. LTV, Borrower attributes e.g. FICO score, Collateral attribute e.g. automobile type etc.
Source of Model's Inputs	Inputs sourced from external and internal sources
Model Outputs	Origination Score

Key Takeaways

- **Model Inventory** is a central repository maintained by the model risk management group but it is the responsibility of the whole organization
- Inventory should be comprehensive and accurate
- Model life stages are: **development, validation, implementation and retirement**
- Information pertaining to all life stages of the model should be captured in the inventory

Chapter 5: Model Risk Rating

"Do not draw your sword to kill a fly."
~ Korean Proverb

Since all models pose varying degrees of risk to an institution, financial institutions assign **Risk Tiers** to categorize them. This helps to prioritize risk management activities to utilize limited resources. For example, models that determine **loan loss reserves** or **loss provision** [7] warrant higher scrutiny compared to a model that determines staffing needs.

Most frequently, models are classified as High, Medium or Low risk. However, either only two or more than three tiers are used by some institutions. The risk rating is usually designed to reflect the potential severity of the financial or reputational loss that could result from an error in or misuse of the model. Given this goal, it is not surprising that risk rating schemas are generally driven by measures of a model's "materiality" (importance) to the institution as well as the model's business "use".

---

[7] Loan loss provision is an expense set aside as an allowance for uncollected loans and loan payments. This provision is used to cover a number of factors associated with potential loan losses including bad loans, customer defaults and renegotiated terms of a loan that incur lower than previously estimated payments.

Materiality Dimension:

Institutions typically try to quantify the **"materiality" dimension** by measuring the size of the assets or loan portfolios to which the model is applied. For example, a bank that has a large portfolio of home mortgages may rate the loss forecasting models related to this portfolio as "high". Similarly, if the bank has a small portfolio of automobile loans, all models related to this portfolio may get a rating of "medium" or "low".

Use Dimension:

When it comes to considering the **"use" dimension**, institutions typically recognize that some model uses are inherently more risky than others. Examples of models considered as 'high' risk include: asset acquisition and dispositions, managing credit or market risk, pricing products, and scoring bank customers based on money laundering risk.

In addition to the materiality and use considerations, institutions sometimes apply other criteria such as model complexity, maturity of the modeling methodology, underlying computational platform (desktop application vs. custom production framework), etc. Models that have inputs or assumptions that are generated by upstream models (other model outputs used as inputs) are also considered more risky. Two different methodologies are described below.

1. Example of Methodology using Use and Materiality as Dimensions

One suggested qualitative inherent risk rating method considers both risk dimensions, i.e. use and materiality, as the primary drivers of the risk rating process. An easy to follow decision tree (Figure 5.1) is used to determine the model's preliminary risk rating (High, Medium or Low).

Under this rating schema, evaluation of the model's risk profile along the "use" dimension occurs in two stages. First, determine if the model measures or forecasts *risk, price* or *value*. A credit underwriting scorecard model to qualify borrowers for loans is an example of a model used to measure *risk*, whereas a model used to price a derivative (call or a put option or other derivative products) is an example of a model that measures *price*. Models used for determining the **value of a loan portfolio**[8] would fall under models used to measure *value*. Most models in a typical financial institution would fall into the category of measuring risk, price or value. Models that do not measure risk, price or value would be automatically assigned to the *Low* risk category.

These include call center staffing models, some types of marketing models, or models that predict which customers are more likely to leave the bank. Assignment of such models to the *Low* risk category is consistent with the minimal financial risk associated with these models.

---

[8] Price that another entity would be willing to pay to transfer the loan portfolio. This is distinct from the outstanding balance.

FIGURE 5.1. Model Risk Rating Methodology using Use and Materiality as Dimensions

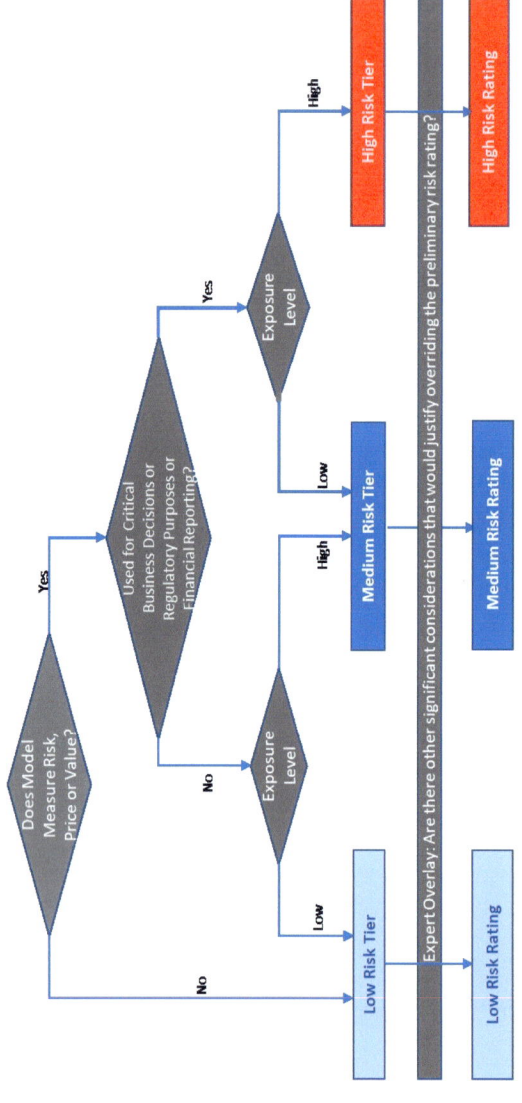

Next, for those models that do measure or forecast *price*, *risk* or *value*, determine if the results from the models are used for critical business decisions, financial reporting or regulatory purposes. Credit risk underwriting scorecards, loss provision, and economic capital models, for example, fall into this category, whereas a loss-forecasting model that is used only for **benchmarking**[9] likely would not. Although there is some degree of subjectivity in determining the criticality of model use, for the majority of models, the assessment based on experience is unequivocal.

Once the *use* of the model is determined, the *exposure*, defined as the size of the portfolio of assets or liabilities to which the model is applied is considered. Models with multiple uses are rated for each use separately, taking into consideration the criticality and exposure for each use. The *exposure* is evaluated against a specific dollar threshold, a first step in the direction of model risk appetite[10], that is set by a governing body based on a percentage of the institution's overall assets and is re-evaluated on a periodic basis.

Once the *preliminary* risk rating is assigned, other factors that may affect the model's risk profile are considered. At times when the portfolio size cannot be defined or, as mentioned above, is not representative of the true inherent risk of the model, a different materiality measure may be considered to adjust the rating upwards or downwards. Any factors that move a model's risk rating away from the rating set by the

---

[9] evaluate or check (something) by comparison with a standard

[10] Risk appetite is the amount and type of risk that an organization is willing to take in order to meet its strategic objectives.

initial decision tree are documented in the model inventory database or other tracking systems.

A final risk rating is assigned to the model by taking into account any other significant considerations that would justify overriding the preliminary rating. For example, trading assets like derivatives would need additional considerations since the notional[11] amount of derivatives may be quite significant. However, the impact due to the market price is expected to be much lower. A final risk rating is obtained through a consensus among all stakeholders including the independent model risk management staff, model developer, and model users.

2. Example of Risk Rating Methodology using additional criteria

Complex risk rating methods may use several factors such as model impact, dependence, limitations, predictive power, governance etc. as shown in Figure 5.2. A score that is purely subjective typically ranges from 0 to 10 (or 5) is assigned to each factor with 10 (or 5) posing the highest risk. The intent of the score is simply to compare one model to another, thus the numeric score range can be arbitrary. Each factor is explained in detail below. Once all factors are scored, a cumulative score is calculated by summing them up. Model risk rating is then assigned by comparing the cumulative scores across models to obtain a desired distribution.

---

[11] The notional amount on a financial instrument is the nominal or face amount that is used to calculate payments made on that instrument.

FIGURE 5.2. Model Risk Rating Methodology using Several Factors

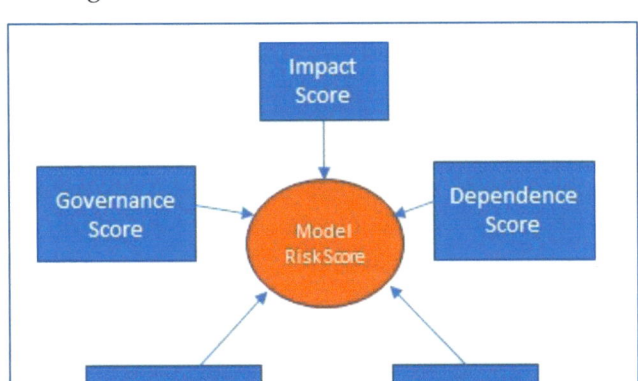

Each of these factors are described below.

Model Impact Factor: The Model Impact factor accounts for the estimated inherent risk of the activity that is modeled including the economic environment, the bank's business practices, and the nature of the decisions or reporting the model supports. This is similar to the materiality factor discussed above. Model Impact factor would depend on model severity and frequency of use. For example, if a proprietary credit underwriting scorecard is used frequently for approving loans for a bank's portfolio that is significant, the model impact factor would be very large compared to a model used for estimating how many customers a bank is likely to lose.

Model Dependence Factor: The Dependence factor accounts for the degree to which the bank's decisions or reporting are impacted by the dependence on the model's output. For example, a model that is used alongside other complementary models, or where the model is an input into a decision that also utilizes management judgment, would have a lower dependence than a model that is used by itself or as part of an automated decision strategy such as the scorecard.

Model Limitations: The Model Limitations category refers to weaknesses in a model due in part to the various shortcomings, approximations, and uncertainties that are unavoidable. Alternatively, weaknesses could result from assumptions underlying a model that may restrict the model's scope to a limited set of specific circumstances and situations. For example, a fundamentally sound model may exhibit high model risk if it is used outside of the environment for which it was designed: for instance applying existing models to new products or markets, or changes to market conditions or customer behaviors.

Model Predictive Power Factor: The assessment of the Model Predictive Power category could include the following subcategories:

- **Back-Test** subcategory: Back-testing refers to tracking a model's output over past time and comparing it to observed values. If back-testing is not possible, sensitivity analysis can be conducted. The model's risk may then be evaluated based on whether back-testing is conducted regularly and how well it follows the past trends of the portfolio.
- **Benchmark** subcategory: Benchmark subcategory refers to the availability of means to benchmark the model's results using appropriate industry sources, how regularly benchmarking is conducted and how well the model performs compared to the benchmark.

- **The Statistical Measure** subcategory refers to how well a given statistical measure reflects the strength of the model, e.g R^2 for a linear regression model.

Model Governance Factor: The Governance category refers to documentation of model development and validation. The assessment of the Governance category should include the following subcategories:

- The **Documentation** subcategory refers to the level of detail of the model documentation to allow parties unfamiliar with a model to understand how the model operates, as well as its limitations and key assumptions. It should show how well the Model is challenged, its control environment, and whether or not the documentation and results are subject to proper levels of review.
- The **Implementation** subcategory refers to the effectiveness of the Model Implementation process. This should include an assessment of whether there is a formalized implementation plan, and associated procedures, in place; whether results are reviewed; and whether model change procedures exist and are being followed.
- The **Operational Controls** subcategory refers to how robust the model control environment is and whether operational controls have been properly identified, implemented and documented.

For example, a model that uses complex theory and has a significant manual aspect in implementation would have a high score. Alternatively, a relatively simple model that has been implemented in a thoroughly tested environment and is automated would get a low risk score. Sometimes, these categories are separated with a risk score in each category.

There are pros and cons to each type of methodology. Whereas the methodology using only use and materiality dimensions may be easier and can result in a risk rating at the time of model identification, the complex risk rating methodology can determine the risk rating of the model only after the validation is complete since many factors can only be determined when the model is reviewed in entirety.

The model's inherent risk rating by itself impacts the scope, depth, and frequency of several model risk mitigation activities as mentioned before. Impacted activities may include the rigor and frequency of independent validation testing, the scope of the annual review, the relative roles and responsibilities of the model owners/developers and the independent model risk management staff with respect to several risk mitigation activities, and so on.

Key Takeaways

- Models are risk rated to prioritize risk management activities
- Model risk rating impacts scope, depth and frequency of model risk mitigation activities
- Banks develop their own risk rating methodologies that can be simple or complex
- Typical risk tiers for model are High, Medium and Low
- Model can be rated using the Use and Materiality approach or using factors such as impact, dependence, limitations, predictive power and governance

Chapter 6: Model Validation

"Risk comes from not knowing what you are doing." – Warren Buffet

Once a model has been identified and/or added to the inventory, the model typically needs to be validated before it is approved for use. As mentioned earlier, model validation is a thorough review of the model. In some instances, a model can be approved for use prior to validation if either it is deemed to be low risk and/or appropriate controls exist that mitigate the risk. In these cases, validation can occur after the model has been in use. Validation process evaluates whether the model is sound and being used for the purpose it was meant for. High risk models are typically validated more frequently than medium or low risk ones.

Best practice suggests that the model validation process should follow standard project management steps as shown below in Figure 6.1:

FIGURE 6.1. Model Validation Process

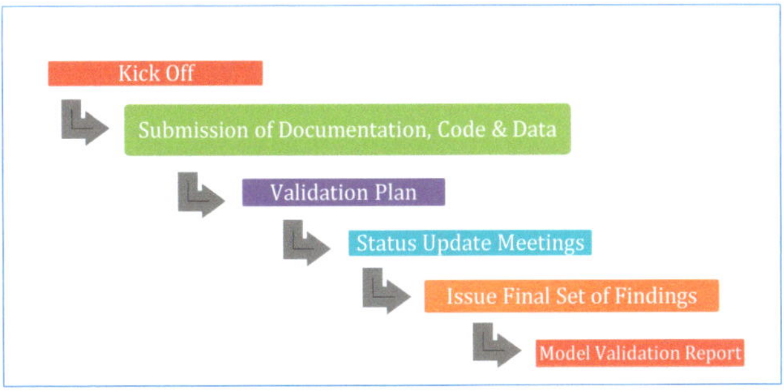

- Kick Off
- Submission of Documentation, Code & Data
- Validation Plan
- Status Update Meetings
- Issue Final Set of Findings
- Model Validation Report

Kick-off: This is the first phase of the project which is essentially a meeting between the model owners and the model validators. At this meeting, model owners provide an overview of the model, including its purpose, methodology, modeling data, implementation platform etc. This gives a chance for the validators to get acquainted with the model and the model owners.

Submission of documentation, code, data: Shortly after kick-off, the model owners provide complete model documentation along with any model development code, modeling data etc. Submission of comprehensive documentation and complete and clean code is imperative for the validation to remain on schedule.

Validation Plan: In this phase, the model validators create a plan for conducting the validation. Typical time required to formulate the plan is approximately 1-2 weeks from the submission of model documentation. During this time, the validators should read the model documentation and prepare a list of additional items required from the model owners (typically called RFI - request for information) that may help with the validation. The list may include supporting documents, additional code and/or data. It is helpful to review the validation plan with senior managers and peers to ensure that the validation team has not missed any area. The validation plan should cover all areas discussed further in the chapter.

Status Update meetings: Regular status update meetings should be scheduled by the validators with the model owners to apprise them of the status of validation. During these meetings, validators may also present any preliminary findings or concerns they have with the model to get clarification etc. instead of waiting till the end to submit formal findings. These meetings ensure that all stake-holders of the validation project are in agreement. This causes minimum interference with model owners' other priorities.

Issue Final Set of Findings: After the completion of model validation, there may still be some unresolved issues or findings identified by the validators. Model validators formalize these findings along with recommendations for resolving the findings with the model owners. After model owners and validators agree to the final set, these findings get finalized.

Model Validation Report: At the conclusion of validation, a report is issued by the validation team. This report should be very comprehensive and should detail all the analysis along with testing etc.

So what does a thorough validation entail? Model validation process follows the typical risk

Managing Risk of Financial Models • 37

management techniques as shown in Figure 6.2 below. As part of validation, model validators identify and assess risk associated with a model and evaluate controls that mitigate the risk. Weaknesses and limitations not identified in the model documentation are also evaluated.

FIGURE 6.2. Model Risk Management Schematic

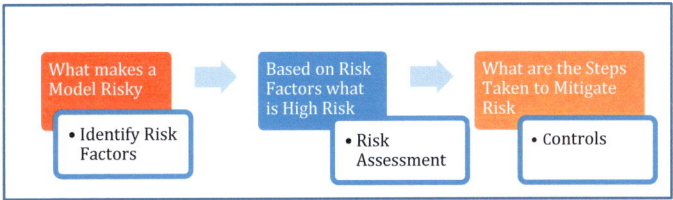

Model risk management practitioners typically cover the five risk components of the model during validation as shown in Figure 6.3. Proper governance or oversight on all components is also essential.

FIGURE 6.3. Components of Model Risk

- Model Data[1]
- Model
- Model Theory[2]
- Testing[4]
- Input Data[1]
- Implementation[3]
- Model Outcomes[4]

Inherent risks in each of these components are described below. Corresponding controls are described later.

1. *Model Data Risk*

Model Data risk, defined as the possibility that either the data used to develop the model or the data that is used as an input to the model at run time ("production data") are inappropriate, incomplete, or inaccurate, can arise from a number of sources including the following ones:

− Using proxy data, such as the data from a different portfolio or even a different institution, to develop the model when the desired data are not available

− Using outdated data that is not representative of the current portfolio to develop the model

− Extracting data from the wrong internal data source, or misunderstanding the definitions of the extracted data fields

− Having errors in the data extraction and manipulation process

− Choosing inappropriate or statistically invalid data sampling or transformation rules, such as imputation of missing values or treatment of outliers

− Biased data due to developer exclusions or design of data sample

− Having inconsistencies between model development and production data.

2. Model Theory Risk

Model Theory risk, defined as the possibility of using inappropriate methodology or assumptions, or model misspecification, can manifest itself in many ways, including (but not limited to):

– Choosing a model development approach that is not suitable for the business problem at hand

– Choosing a statistical estimation technique that is not appropriate for the business problem or the available development data

– Employing modeling assumptions that are inappropriate or incorrect

– Using input variables that do not have logical business relationships with the dependent variable, omitting important variables from the model, or including multiple highly correlated independent variables

– Incorrect functional forms and presence of statistical or econometric flaws

– Over-fitting the model to development data

3. Model Implementation Risk

Model Implementation risk is defined as the possibility that the production implementation of the model is mathematically inaccurate or inconsistent with the development version of the model. The factors that are considered include:

– Complexity of the application

– Transparency of the calculations (e.g. vendor model "black box" vs. internally developed C++ / JAVA / SAS™ code), computational platform

(spreadsheet-based application with hundreds of difficult to audit formulas vs. SAS™ programming code)
– Number of production data feeds
– Whether the application is implemented by the model developer or a separate IT group, as well as other factors

Another consideration is if the code is structured in a way to reduce the risk of updates (e.g. by using macro-variables for assumptions or settings) and to provide transparency to model calculations

4. *Model Outcomes & Uncertainty Risk*

The Model Outcomes and Uncertainty Risk reflects the possibility that model outputs are biased, lack acceptable predictive power or are subject to a great degree of uncertainty. To determine the risk posed by a given model, we carefully consider the characteristics of the model as well as any known information about its performance, including the following factors:

– Whether the model can be back-tested

– Whether the model is designed to predict or measure a common event (e.g. a consumer loan default) or an extremely rare occurrence (e.g. a major market disruption)

– Whether the model can be benchmarked to other models or other available information

– Existence of known weaknesses in the model's performance (e.g. significant back-testing errors)

– Whether the model's estimates are subject to significant degree of uncertainty due to specific design features (e.g. using static backward-looking assumptions to drive long-term forecasts)

– Whether the model is dependent on judgmental assumptions that can significantly alter model outputs (e.g. House Price Appreciation forecasts)

– Whether the variable being modeled is known to be forecastable at the modeled level (e.g. equity prices, house price turning points, etc.)

5. *Model Governance and Use Risk*

Model Governance and Misuse risk category covers four distinct types of risks that are associated with the post-implementation use of the model:

– The risk that the model outputs or the model itself will be misused by the users,

– The risk that an operational error, including the use of incorrect settings and assumptions, will cause the model run to produce erroneous results,

– The risk that unapproved/incorrect model assumptions are used,

– The risk that change management and version control procedures are not followed appropriately.

To assess the likelihood that an operational error might occur, a number of factors are considered, including the following ones:

– Whether the model application is deployed in a controlled IT environment,

– The maturity of the production process,

– The complexity of the production process in terms of the number of model components that have to be separately executed, the number of data hand-offs between components, as well as the number and complexity of the data feeds,

– The degree of automation of the production process, including getting model assumptions and setting into the model application in an automated fashion rather than through manual user input,

– Existence and the number of settings and assumptions that must be updated frequently as part of the normal course of model use.

Measuring the risk that the model output may be misused requires considering the nature of this output and all possible ways that it can be used. Some models have an inherently narrow and specific purpose, such as a model that calculates a fraud risk score for bank customers. Other models present users with an almost irresistible opportunity to apply their outputs to other problems. For example, models designed to predict probabilities of default using **through-the-cycle**[12] estimation should not be used for business forecasting and budgeting which should depend on macroeconomic factors.

---

[12] These models do not depend on any macroeconomic factors as opposed to point-in-time that do use. Typically, models that score borrowers for credit underwriting purposes do not use macroeconomic factors since all borrowers will be subject to same conditions.

In other words, output of a model should not be considered a commodity but be used for a bespoke purpose.

The section below describes several controls associated with each of the areas of model risk.

1. Model Data Control

Model data risk can be mitigated by several key controls as listed below:

– Verification of the development data accuracy and completeness by the model developers. Examples include reconciliation reports and testing for accuracy on a sample of underlying data

– Documentation and testing of the appropriateness of the development data by the model developers in the situations when proxy data are used

– Detailed and comprehensive documentation of the data extraction, scrubbing, transformation, and sampling rules with justification of the reasons for the choices made by the developers

– Documentation and testing of the consistency of the production and model development data

– Controls around the source data stored in the corporate data warehouse designed to ensure data accuracy

– Operational controls around the production data extraction and manipulation designed to ensure completeness and integrity of the production data.

2. Model Theory Control

Model theory risk can be mitigated by several controls as listed below:

– Detailed documentation on the appropriateness of the selected theoretical approach and statistical estimation technique (if applicable), including an assessment of alternative methodologies / techniques with the associated pros and cons

– Comprehensive testing of statistical validity, stability, fit, and robustness of the model by the developers,

– Detailed documentation supporting the appropriateness of the key modeling assumptions, including testing of alternative assumptions and analysis of sensitivity of model outputs to assumption changes or violations of existing assumptions,

– Use of a structured empirically-based approach for selecting variables for inclusion in the model as opposed to an ad hoc judgmental approach (if feasible). Documentation explaining the logical business relationships between the input variables and the dependent variable, and support for any variable transformations.

3. *Model Implementation Control*

Model Implementation Risk can be mitigated by the following controls:

– Selection of an inherently more transparent implementation platform (e.g. SAS™ vs. Excel)

– Development of the production code in a manner that increases its transparency and reduces redundancy, as well as inclusion of copious comments within the code explaining the logic

– Development of the production model in a manner that minimizes the need for on-going changes to the production code. One approach is to separate the portion of the model containing parameters and assumptions requiring periodic updates into a self-contained module

– Rigorous, structured, and well documented testing of the production implementation by the developers, users, and (if applicable) IT production team. Using a development version of the model or a testing emulator to tie out to the production outputs is one of the most robust methods for testing implementation accuracy

– Maximum use of models that have been widely tested by other institutions (typically vendor models), providing that all other risk mitigation controls have been employed as well

– Testing of the consistency of the production data feeds with the model development data (if applicable).

4.   Model Outcomes & Uncertainty Control

Model Outcomes and Uncertainty Risk can be mitigated by the following:

– Sufficiently frequent, rigorous, and well documented on-going periodic testing of model performance through back-testing, sensitivity analysis including stress and boundary condition testing, and benchmarking to other models

– Explicit measurement of model uncertainty, communication of uncertainty measures to the model users, and incorporation of the uncertainty measures into the model output

– Application of conservatism principle when selecting model assumptions and parameters or when using the model outputs

- Developing robust risk mitigants for model weaknesses and limitations that are known to increase the uncertainty

- To the extent that the model is very sensitive to uncertain assumptions, such as forecasts of macro-economic factors, increasing the oversight over such assumptions.

A point to note is that performance monitoring requires an effective governance process with clearly defined roles and responsibilities. It is not enough that back-testing is performed; appropriate reviews are essential.

5.   *Model Governance and Use Control*

Model Governance and Use Risk can be mitigated by the following:

- Implementation of operational controls by model owners and testing of operational controls by independent testing group. Controls should cover the following areas:
  - Prevention of unauthorized use of the model,
  - Prevention of unauthorized changes to the model,
  - Prevention of the use of unapproved assumptions and parameters,
  - Testing of completeness and accuracy of model inputs and intermediate results at every data hand-off,
  - Assessment of the reasonability of model outputs.

- Automation of production model implementation to reduce the number of manual steps and data hand-offs,
- Moving models from the developer-owned environment to IT-controlled production environment subject to uniform control standards.

There are instances when validators identify issues (risks), sometimes referred to as findings where model risk is identified but not mitigated through controls. Validators then make recommendations to address the findings. These issues or findings are also tracked in the model inventory and described in the following section. More information on how to word effective findings and issue recommendations is described in Chapter 7.

SR 11-7 also requires that all models undergo an annual review in the year it is not validated to ensure that the model is performing satisfactorily. An annual review can be considered as a light validation where predominantly model outcomes are reviewed.

After a validation is performed, a validation report is produced elucidating the scope of review of the model, review of model documentation for accuracy and completeness, various tests conducted, independent analyses or challenger models developed by the validation team, etc.

Chapter 7 shows how such findings and associated recommendations can be managed effectively is described.

Key Takeaways

- Model validation process should follow standard project management practice
- Model validation areas include: development data, theory, output, implementation, and governance
- Validators evaluate risks in each area and associated mitigating controls
- As a result of validations, model validators issue findings, the remediation of which is expected to mitigate model risk

Chapter 7: Findings and Recommendations

"We all need people who will give us feedback. That's how we improve." ~ Bill Gates

As mentioned in the previous section, recommendations may come out of any oversight or review activity that the Model Risk Management Group conducts including validations, performance monitoring review, annual reviews, or governance activities. Majority of recommendations arise from validations since the entire model is reviewed at that time. Annual reviews mostly result in findings related to model performance.

When issuing the findings, validators should attempt to formulate the findings that are relatively self-contained since they typically will be extracted from a report and saved in the database and thus need to be understood on their own. Recommendations for remediation of the findings should be "**SMART**" (Specific, Measurable, Achievable, Relevant, Time-bound), as well as concise (typically a recommendation will be shorter than the associated finding).

FIGURE 7.1. SMART recommendations

> **S**pecific
> **M**easurable
> **A**chievable
> **R**elevant
> **T**ime-bound

The creator of a recommendation should clearly state how the recommendation could be closed. Open-ended recommendations should be avoided, although some latitude should be allowed as to the approach taken.

Each recommendation is typically assigned a criticality. Criticality is categorized as High, Medium, and Low or Tier 1, 2, 3 respectively. Documenting the rationale for the criticality assignment is also considered good practice so that other similar findings are rated consistently.

All recommendations, along with associated target completion/remediation dates, are discussed with the responsible party (model owner) prior to being issued, and follow applicable procedures and approval processes at the institution. In some institutions, recommendations may need to be approved by a committee; in others they can be approved by the head of model risk or a senior member of the validation department. At some institutions, recommendations are treated as official if there is a consensus between the model owner and the validation team. If there is no consensus, the matter may be escalated to a committee.

The validation recommendations lifecycle is illustrated in Figure 7.2.

The typical high-level recommendation resolution procedure is described below.

1. Once issued, findings and recommendations are entered in the recommendations tracking database along with the associated recommendation target completion dates.

2. Model owner submits remediation materials.

3. The Model Risk Management responsible party reviews the material following guidance below and assesses if the finding can be closed by the resolution date.

FIGURE 7.2. Recommendation Lifecycle

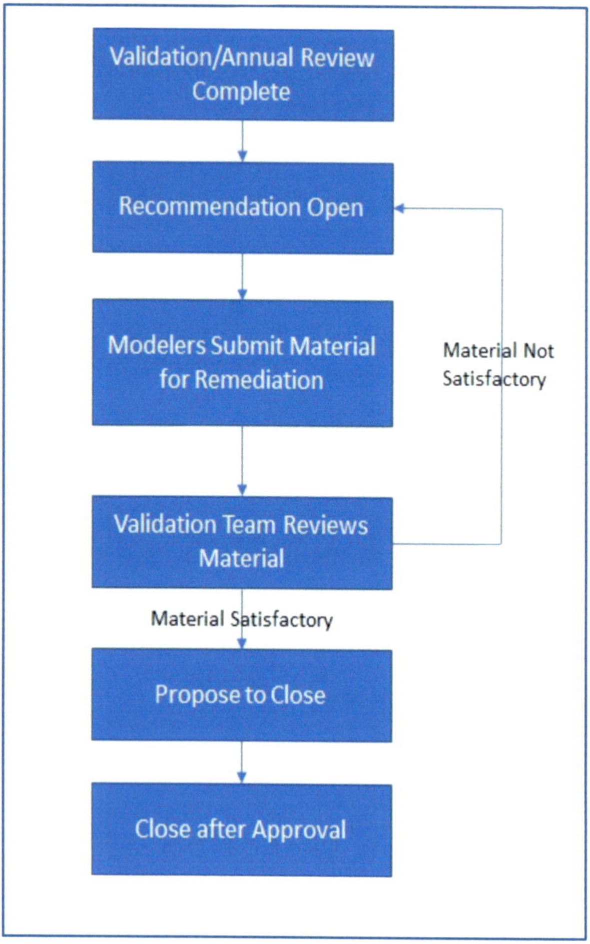

4. The proposed status of a recommendation after review can be one of the following:

    a. Closed. Materials presented to Model Risk team indicate satisfactory remediation of the finding.

    b. Open. Materials presented to Model Risk team do not indicate satisfactory remediation of the finding.

    c. Risk Accepted (in some cases). Management to accept risk. This status is used in some institutions where cost benefit analysis indicates that the finding may not be resolved and line of business accepts the risk. This typically is allowed for Low criticality findings.

5. Once the proposed status is determined, Model Risk team documents the rationale for the proposed status in the tracking database.

6. All supporting artifacts associated with a recommendation from either the responsible party are archived.

Table 7.1 shows suggested field names that are typically included in the model inventory related to the findings tracking. This list is not comprehensive but merely suggest elements that are considered best practices. Fields can be added or removed as appropriate

TABLE 7.1 Suggested Model Inventory Fields Related to Findings and Recommendations

Field Name	Comments
Finding Number	
Finding Area	Documentation, Data, Theory etc.
Finding Description	
Recommendation	Description for the how the finding can be resolved
Target Date for Resolution	Date by which model owner needs to submit resolution of the finding
Recommendation Status	Open, Closed etc.
Validator Name	
Finding Criticality	High, Medium, Low or Tier 1, Tier 2 etc.
Comments	Rationale for assigning Criticality
Model Owner Resolution Description	Description of how model owner proposes to resolve finding
Attachment from Model Owner supporting resolution	Place to attach any supporting document for resolution
Validator Comments	Rationale for closing the finding
Resolution Date	

Key Takeaways

- Findings resulting from model reviews should be saved in a database
- Findings should be relatively self-contained
- Recommendations to address the findings should be SMART – Specific, Measurable, Achievable, Relevant, and Time-Bound
- Evidence submitted by the model owners to the validators to remediate findings should be carefully evaluated and archived before closing the finding

Chapter 8: Templates for Documentation and Validation

"Proper Planning and Preparation Prevents Poor Performance." ~ Steven Keague

Model documentation that is clear and comprehensive is critical not only for validation, but also for ongoing use and refinement. Since model validation team reviews the model documentation for its compliance with SR 11-7, it is beneficial if the model risk management develops a **template**[13] that all model owners can use when they develop model documentation. The sections that should be included cover all the aspects of model validation such as model data, theory, outcomes analysis, implementation, and mode governance. Similarly, the model risk management group should also develop templates for their validation reports for consistency and completeness. The following sections are recommended as shown in Figure 8.1.

---

[13] A template is a file that serves as a starting point for a new document. It is pre-formatted in some way.

FIGURE 8.1. Table of Contents for Model Documentation

Table of Contents	
	1. Executive Summary
	2. Model Purpose
	3. Model Data
	4. Model Design and Theory
	5. Model Specification and Estimation
	6. Model Testing
	7. Model Implementation
	8. Model Monitoring
	9. Model Operational Controls

Each of these sections is described below.

1. Executive Summary

Documentation should begin with an executive summary, which consists of a high-level synthesis of the sections covered in the following paragraphs. The executive summary should include the model name and version number, the intent of the model and reason for development, the benefits of the model, a brief description of the methodology used, main input variables, implementation method, and a high-level appraisal of the model performance.

2. Model Purpose

This section should include a clear and complete description of what is being modeled, along with the business context for the model's use and impact (e.g. the portfolio size, the amount intended to be originated as loans, and how the model will support decision making, etc.). The range of appropriate application should also be listed with special focus on products or underliers covered by the model.

3. Model Data

This section should describe the sources, nature, and manner by which data was collected and prepared, including any cleansing, filtering, or other transformations used to construct the data upon which the model is built. The reasonableness and appropriateness of data sources should be explained.

Any judgmental and/or qualitative aspects of the independent variable definitions, and/or the sampling approach and sample design should be documented as should the support the treatment of missing data.

In summary, all aspects of data used for modeling purposes should be discusses to support appropriateness, completeness, and accuracy.

4. Model Design and Theory

This section should describe the model methodology at a level of mathematical detail that would enable an experienced modeler to reproduce the key outputs – programming code is not considered as an alternative to documentation of the model methodology.

The model design consists of the selection of a set of inputs, and a process by which the inputs are combined to produce an output.

The design, theory, and logic underlying the model must be well documented and generally supported by published research and sound industry practice. References to literature to support theory, where available, are also expected to be provided.

5. Model Specification and Estimation

This section should include a description of the numerical techniques and implementation choices used to specify and calibrate the final model.

Variable selection and transformation process should be described along with justification. Anticipated relationships of independent variables on the dependent variable are also expected to be provided. This helps the reader understand why those particular variables prevent modelers from using variables identified from data mining resulting in spurious correlation.

Documentation should include discussions that ensure the segments created are of sufficient size to allow meaningful statistical models to be built. If applicable, intermediate and alternative model specifications should be documented, including a description of why the final specification was chosen.

6. Model Testing

All model tests done during development should be included in this section.

If applicable, the model results should be compared to benchmark or alternative models and, if there are any biases or divergence between the predictions, one should provide commentary on the analysis in this section.

Testing should include sensitivity testing, evaluating the behavior of the model under a range of hypothetical scenarios ("what-if" type scenarios, also known as predictable consequences tests) etc.

7. Model Implementation

This section should describe the implementation test plan and results used by developers to ensure that the model that is developed and validated is the same model that is implemented.

While the implementation test plan may differ, depending on model type and complexity, typically, implementation testing documentation includes:

a. A description of model implementation requirements, and the scope of implementation testing.
b. A description of the tests to be performed.
c. A description of the test case set.
d. A list of all output fields that are used for benchmarking regression testing.

e. The degree of tolerance for deviance in the test results.
f. A discussion by the model owners of the sufficiency of the implementation test plan considering the model's purpose and the complexity of the model.

SR 11-7 also expects model owners are required to develop user and operating manuals to ensure that comprehensive procedures are created to limit all aspects of model risk.

8. **Model Monitoring**

SR 11-7 guidance suggests that the results of each model be monitored to ensure that the model continues to be robust (explained in chapter 9). Model monitoring plan should include model monitoring design and review protocols, including the frequency of review, triggers, escalation procedures, and the handling of overrides.

9. **Model Operational Controls**

This section should describe the operational controls (e.g. password protection for Excel spreadsheets, secure access to a web application etc.) used to ensure that the models are correctly implemented and continue to function as intended.

Key Takeaways

- Model documentation that is consistent for all models used at a financial institution facilitates model validations
- For consistent documentation, it is most efficient if documentation templates are provided by model risk management departments
- Templates should be comprehensive and should cover all the areas of model validation

Chapter 9: Model Monitoring

"This leaves the thorny and controversial issue of ongoing monitoring for a later stage."
~ Sergey Lavrov

The regulatory guidance requires ongoing monitoring of models to confirm that the models are appropriately implemented and used, and performing as intended. Model monitoring is performed by the model users and/or the model development team.

Models that belong to the forecasting group are often best monitored by comparing forecasts to actual outcomes – "back-tests." In situations when back-tests are not practical or possible, benchmarking model outputs against alternative but related models can be used. Where appropriate, goodness-of-fit statistics also form a core of useful monitoring data. In all cases, the tracking of values (model outputs), key parameter sensitivities, overrides, and related decision metrics is required (*e.g.* approval rates, booking rates, etc.).

Model Monitoring usually includes four components: **monitoring plan**, **escalation plan**, **trend analysis**, and **out-of-model adjustments and overrides**. These components are outlined below:

1. **Monitoring plan**

   The monitoring plan includes frequency of monitoring that is determined by the complexity, criticality, and frequency of model use. Monitoring is typically conducted on a quarterly basis for models used frequently for business decisions. SR 11-7 guidance requires monitoring to be no less than once per year. The monitoring plan should also include the definition of the variable to be monitored and mathematical specification of the metrics and tests to be used.

2. **Escalation Plan**

   Escalation plan specifies actions that the model owners are expected to take depending on model performance. Since there is a multitude of models in a financial institution's inventory, the model performance monitoring is usually standardized using an escalation process to enable comparison of model performances to one another.

Table 9.1 describes a three-tiered escalation response framework. Model users specify and justify the thresholds separating these tiers.

TABLE 9.1 Model Performance Monitoring Escalation Response Framework

Model Performance Monitoring Escalation Response	
Tier	Response
One	None, model operating acceptably.
Two	Notification to Senior Management and Model Risk Management Group.
Three	Notification with specific recommended response to the Model Risk Management Group and the Model Risk Management Committee.

3. **Trend Analysis**

   An effective model is expected to have a stable performance over time. Trend analysis consists of assessing the evolution of key monitored metrics over time. If the model performance starts to deteriorate, trend analysis provides an early indication of expected future performance.

4. **Out-of-model adjustments and Overrides**

   Since the model results contain uncertainties, out-of-model or on-top adjustments are sometimes conducted to mitigate the model's weaknesses. If not clearly identified, such adjustments may mask model performance issues and underlying model weaknesses. Another category refers to model overrides.

An example of an override is, suppose a proprietary score is used for approving loans with a specified cutoff - meaning all borrowers that have scores below the cutoff are expected to be declined. If some borrowers are accepted despite having a score lower than the cutoff, such cases should also be monitored.

Key Takeaways

- All models used at a financial institution should be monitored and results provided to the model risk management department
- A model monitoring plan should be included as part of the model documentation and should include relevant metrics with tiers and escalation plan associated with each tier
- Model monitoring should be conducted according to the plan and should include trend analysis to evaluate model performance over time
- Out of model adjustments and overrides should be assessed and documented

Chapter 10: Model Risk Reporting

"The first step in good reporting is good snooping." ~ Matt Drudge

The regulatory guidance places the ultimate responsibility for managing institution's model risk on the Board of Directors and senior management. According to SR 11-7, "[The model risk management] framework should be grounded in an understanding of model risk — not just for individual models but also in the aggregate." Having a quantitative measure of model risk for each model in the institution's inventory allows management to view the aggregate level of risk across the institution or for any group of models. Management might be interested in understanding the level of overall model risk in each business unit or functional area of the institution. Additionally, management may be interested in evaluating the aggregate level of risk across all models, but limited to a particular risk area, e.g. data risk, or on-going use risk. Alternatively, they may want to examine model risk concentrations within each of the institution's critical analytical frameworks that rely on multiple models, for example, the Allowance for Loan and Lease Loss estimation, Regulatory and Economic Capital Adequacy Assessment frameworks, Asset and Liability Management framework, etc.

For estimating aggregate model risk, the model risk management team creates reports that focus on various aspects discussed above. The reports can be divided into following areas:

1. Model Risk Rating Distribution

The report in this area shows the distribution of models in each risk rating. The reports typically show the distribution of models for the whole bank and within each business unit. This report is important because it shows whether model risk rating methodology is reasonable. It also helps in determining staffing needs for model risk management.

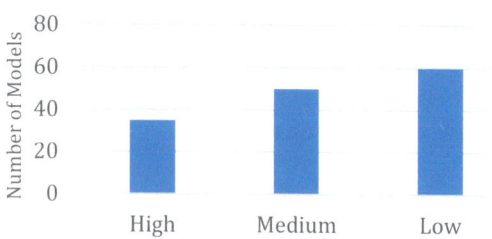

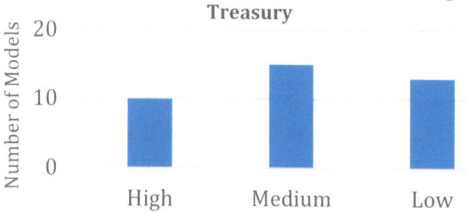

2. Model Validation Status

A sample report on model validation status by business units is shown below:

Business Unit	Model Risk Rating	Validation up to date	Validation overdue	Never Validated	Total
Overall	High	35	5	5	40
	Medium	50	6	4	60
	Low	60	0	0	60
Overall Total		145	11	9	160
Treasury	High	10	2	3	15
	Medium	15	1	1	17
	Low	13	0	0	13
Treasury Total		38	3	4	45
Consumer Banking	High	...	...	...	...
	Medium	...	...	...	...
	Low	...	...	...	...

Such a report is useful to gauge whether the model validation group is adequately staffed to perform all model risk management activities according to schedule. This report is also important to assess whether the risk appetite of the bank is being breached etc.

3. Open Model Findings Based on Business Units

A sample report on open findings by business units is shown below:

Business Unit	Model Risk Rating	High Criticality	Medium Criticality	Low Criticality	Total
Overall	High	35	5	5	40
	Medium	50	6	4	60
	Low	60	0	0	60
Overall Total		145	11	9	160
Treasury	High	10	2	3	15
	Medium	15	1	1	17
	Low	13	0	0	13
Treasury Total		38	3	4	45

This report indicates whether the open findings are concentrated in a particular business unit. This report is also important to assess whether the risk appetite of the bank is being breached etc.

4. Model Findings Based on Validation Areas

This report shows the distribution of open findings by validation areas. A sample report is shown below:

Business Unit	Model Risk Rating	High Criticality	Medium Criticality	Low Criticality	Total
Overall	High	35	5	5	40
	Medium	50	6	4	60
	Low	60	0	0	60
Overall Total		145	11	9	160
Model Data Findings	High	10	2	3	15
	Medium	15	1	1	17
	Low	13	0	0	13
Model Data Findings Total		38	3	4	45
Model Theory Findings	High	5	2	3	15
	Medium	5	1	1	17
	Low	1	0	0	13
Model Theory Findings Total		11	3	4	45

This report indicates whether the model risk identified in the form of findings is being mitigated appropriately. This report can highlight any themes that arise out of validations. For example, if there is a large number of open findings related to data, the bank may want to invest in better data warehouses or if there are several findings in model theory, the models may be weak etc.

The tables shown above are just some examples of reports that management may be interested in to evaluate the effectiveness of the model risk management program. Model risk management programs continue to evolve in each institution depending on maturity of the program. Model risk management also must be flexible to align with any new regulatory guidance.

Key Takeaways

- Model risk reporting allows management to view the aggregate level of risk across the institution or for any group of models.
- Useful reports include the distribution of models based on their risk, validation status of models overall and by line of business and number of open findings
- Model risk reporting is important in evaluating the risk appetite of an institution

Chapter 11: Hypothetical Case Study

"If you can't explain it simply, you don't understand it well enough" – Albert Einstein

To bring it all together, let us consider a case study of a model. Suppose Bank A has been underwriting all their automobile loans manually. It considers FICO® score of the borrower and loan-to-value of the car and has a policy in place for considering other factors such as payment-to-income ratio or debt-to-income ratio in order to approve/decline the loans which are evaluated by loan officers. This underwriting method worked well earlier in the days when there were few lenders and time was not an issue.

Due to intense competition from other banks and Financial Technology (FinTech) companies that exist now - along with low margins, the bank realizes that it needs to have a more efficient system. The bank notes that most auto originations are indirect originations at dealerships as opposed to direct where the customer walks into a bank looking for a loan. The bank decides to have an automated process which can be accessed by dealers and result in a faster approval process through risk ranking customers based on their credit risk.

The bank has accumulated internal data over five years. The bank decides to build a credit underwriting scorecard using statistical techniques by considering factors such as borrower FICO® score, loan-to-value of the car, resale value of the car, payment-to-income of the borrower etc. The bank uses logistic regression as described in Chapter 6.

Is it a model?

Putting on the hat of a risk manager, the first thing to consider is whether this scorecard is a model. Chapter 3 described guidelines to decide whether a quantitative process is a model as shown below:

Consideration	Assessment	Result
Is considerable subjective judgment exercised at various stages of development, implementation, use, or validation?	There is no clear set of inputs and the modeler is free to choose any variables that best determine rank ordering of borrowers as long as the variables comply with Fair Lending. The process is clearly subjective.	✓
Does the process take an input related to assumptions or data to the "process"?	FICO score, loan-to-value etc. are inputs	✓
Does the process transform inputs into estimates using a quantitative technique?	Here, the inputs are transformed into a score using logistic regression which is a quantitative process.	✓
Does the process produce quantitative	The modeler chose variables that gave	✓

| estimates of uncertain values? (not definitive outputs based on fixed or prescribed calculations) | best results given the underlying data that was used to build the model. On a different development data, the model could easily have yielded different set of coefficients. | |

Since each box is checked, the method is deemed a model.

Addition to the model inventory

Typically, the line of business in-charge of the model notifies the Model Risk Management Group about this process and the model is added to the inventory with the fields filled out for the section on General Model Information and Stage I: Model Development as follows. Since the model has not been validated or implemented the information on Stages II-VI is blank.

Group	Field Name	Comments
General Model Information	Model ID	123
	Model Version	1.0
	Model Name	Auto Origination Scorecard
	Model Status	In development

Stage I: Model Development	Date Added to the Inventory	7/15/2016
	Application Environment	SAS, Excel
	Development: Internal/External	Internal
	Model Type	Statistical
	Model Owner Name	Jane Doe
	Model Owner Group	Retail banking
	Model Purpose/Product(s)	Origination
	Model Developer Name	John Smith
	Model Development Group	Statistical Modeling Center
	Model Development Completion Date	10/31/2016
	Type of Model's Inputs	Borrower and collateral related attributes
	Source of Model's Inputs	Internal
	Model Outputs	Score
Stage II: Model Validation	Model Risk Rating	High
	Model Validator	John Doe
	Validation: Internal/External	Internal
	Date of Last Validation	N/A
	Date of Next Expected Validation	8/31/2017
	Date of Last Annual Review	N/A
	Date of Next Expected Annual Review	8/31/2018

	Model Validation Status	In Validation
	Approval Conditions	
	Model Use Limitations	
	Data Limitations	
	Exceptions to Policy	
Stage III: Model Implementation	**Date Model Implemented**	
Stage IV: In Use	Date Model Went "In Use"	
	Approved Model Use(s)	
	Model User (Contact Person)	
	Model User Group	
	Date of Last Annual Review	
Stage V: Discontinued	**Date Discontinued**	
	Reason Discontinued	
	Attachments: Reason Discontinued	
Attestation	**Attestation: Model Owner**	
	Attestation: Manager Level Approval	
	Attestation: Date	

Model Risk Rating

The next thing to consider is how much the bank risks by relying on this scorecard to approve loans through an automated process. Since the bank's underwriting has been manual and the proposed process has no human intervention, the risk appears to be high. But let us go through a formal process of risk rating this loan. For simplicity let us focus on the first method that uses the flowchart (Figure 5.1 replicated from Chapter 5).

Starting at the top of the flow chart, it is clear that the model does measure risk. So, we go to the right branch of the flow chart (highlighted). The second question is if it is used for critical business decisions and the answer is yes again, so we again go to the right (highlighted). Then comes the exposure level. Let us assume that the threshold set by a governing body based on a percentage of the institution's overall assets is 2.5% and that the exposure of this portfolio currently is 2%. Hence, the exposure would be considered low and we would traverse to the left branch (highlighted). However, since the bank is planning to grow its auto business and is expected to go over 2.5% threshold, an expert overlay is applied and the model is given a final risk rating of "High."

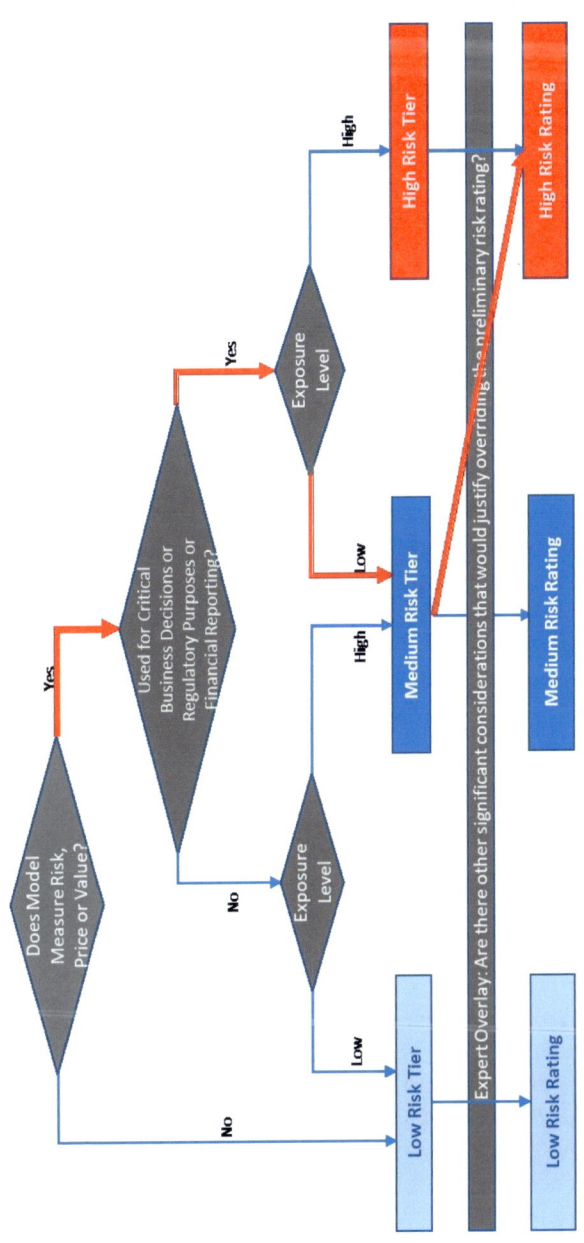

Model Validation

The developed model calculates a risk score based on the probability of default (PD) of auto loans in the next 12 months for use in credit underwriting. The model does not use any macroeconomic factors such as unemployment rate or GDP. The model is statistically estimated using a **Logistic regression technique**[14] based on five years of internal loan performance data. SAS™ software is used to prepare the development data and to perform statistical estimation.

Once the model is built, the model development team creates model documentation using the template created by the Model Risk Management department as explained in Chapter 8. Since by the bank policy, the model cannot be implemented until validated by the model risk management team, the development team submits the model documentation and all the associated code and data for independent validation. Validation is then kicked-off. As mentioned in Chapter 6, the model validation team reviews the model as following.

<u>Model Data Risk</u>: Modeling data is extracted from multiple internal data warehouse tables and is subjected to moderate amount of cleaning and

---

[14] A statistical method for analyzing a dataset in which there are one or more independent variables that determine an outcome. The outcome is measured with a dichotomous variable (in which there are only two possible outcomes). In this particular case, the outcomes are default vs. no default.

transformation before being used in the estimation. Given the fact that the modeling data is from the same portfolio to which the model will be applied in production, and given the fact that a sufficiently long performance history is available, the risk of development data being inappropriate is very low. However, some of the data contains missing values, which have been filled using averages.

Model Data Controls: From the controls perspective, independent assessment of the model owner's controls related to data extraction, merging, scrubbing, sampling, and transformations did not reveal any issues. However, given the missing values were filled using averages, the validation team may issue a finding for the model owner to assess the impact of treating the missing values by other methods such as truncating the missing data, treating missing values by keeping the same variance as opposed to same average etc.

Model Theory Risk and Control: Industry methodologies for developing credit-underwriting scorecards are mature and relatively straightforward. Logistic regression is a common and accepted statistical estimation technique of choice for this model type. Model structure choices are well informed by empirical data, and the degree of required developer judgment is relatively low. Validation team's evaluation of the model owner's support for the model theory and assumptions raised no concerns. The model does not rely on exogenous assumptions, such as economic forecasts.

A review of the model theory, assumptions, estimation process, and final model structure did not result in any notable issues, hence the validation team feels that the Model Theory risk was fully mitigated. Model validation team does not issue any findings in this area.

Model Outcomes and Uncertainty Risk: Given the short-term nature of the model forecast (12 months) the overall level of model uncertainty is relatively lower to begin with. The model is back-testable, and the available model fit analysis demonstrates low error and very high ability of the model to rank-order loans by risk level on both out-of-sample and out-of-time tests. These factors suggest that the risk of model predictions being biased is low. However, the model is applied to an auto portfolio data, and the validation team considers the auto market to be fairly volatile, even when only a 12-month period is considered. Additionally, shifts in the bank's strategies can lead to rapid changes in actual default rates that may not be captured by the model trained on historical data.

Model Outcomes and Uncertainty Controls: While all the tests of historical model fit suggest high model accuracy, market volatility factors leads the validation team to the conclusion that the uncertainty risk is only partially mitigated. Model validation team may issue a finding asking the model owners to conduct additional sensitivity tests to ensure that the model responds appropriately to factors relevant to the auto portfolio such as debt-to-income and loan to value (LTV) which might be affected by strategy.

Model Implementation Risk: The model is internally developed using SAS™ and implemented within a SAS™ production platform. The complexity of the implementation is very low; the production application performs data extraction and preparation and then applies a single equation to calculate each loan's credit score. Due to the use of a clearly readable scripting language to encode the production model, the implementation is highly transparent and easy to test.

Model Implementation Controls: The model owner and users performed extensive pre-implementation testing of the model production system that was documented in a comprehensive manner. Model validation team performed testing of the implementation by building a complete independent replica of the system and obtaining identical outputs, which confirmed the effectiveness of the model owner's controls. Model validation team does not issue any findings.

Model Governance and Use Risk: The model resides within a production platform provided by SAS™, but is not subject to IT General controls. Running the model does not require any manual data feeding or setting of parameters and assumption. The process is fully automated from start to finish and requires the user only to initiate it. Consequently, the risk of operational errors is fairly low. The risk of misinterpretation of the model outputs -- loan level risk scores -- is also very low. However, no change management process exists.

Model Governance and Use Controls: Operational controls around the production application designed to prevent unauthorized use of the model provides a strong mitigation for this risk area. Validation team's review of the controls does not identify any notable weaknesses. However, since there is no change management process for implementing any model change, even authorized personnel may change the production code without the knowledge of other stakeholders. Validation team issues a finding related to the absence of the change management process.

The example above shows at a high level, how the validation of a model should be conducted with suggestions on issuing findings and recommendations for remediation.

Findings and Recommendations

Based on the validation process described above, the model validation team issues the following findings along with recommendations.

Finding Area	Finding Criticality	Finding Description	Recommendation	Target Date
Model Data	Medium	The missing values were filled using averages reducing the variance of the risk factor.	Assess the impact of treating the missing values by other methods such as truncating the missing data, treating missing values by keeping the same variance as opposed to	12/31/2017

			same average etc	
Model Outcomes and Uncertainty	Medium	No sensitivity tests were conducted	Demonstrate through sensitivity testing whether the model is appropriately sensitive to factors such as LTV and debt-to-income	12/31/2017
Model Governance and Use	Medium	No change management exists	Implement and document a change management process to ensure that any change in the model notified to all stakeholders	12/31/2017

The example presented above hopefully provides an insight into how a model is incorporated into the Model Risk Management system of a bank.

Model Risk Management is an exciting evolving field. From the earlier days of model validation, financial institutions have made immense progress where the whole model lifecycle is tracked. Even community banks, insurance and financial technology companies are beginning to establish model risk management programs to have governance on models used for making critical decisions. Risk Management function of banks now track model risk along with credit, market and operational risk. For capital planning and CCAR submissions, model risk management has become imperative.

The team members in this field are subject matter experts, quantitative analysts, project managers, and people who are critical thinkers and curious who think outside the box. Hopefully this book has provided you with an overview of the intricacies of a strong model risk management program.

Acknowledgements

There are many individuals who played a significant role in making this book possible. First and foremost, I would like to thank Sanjeev Mankotia who introduced me to Model Risk Management. I was fortunate to co-author a paper with him that was published in Risk Management Journal in July/August 2013. I would also like to thank my supervisor Doug Gardner who constantly challenges me in every model validation with thoughtful insights.

My sister, Sunanda Chatterjee, my husband, Arun Majumdar, my daughter, Shalini Majumdar, and my brother, Jayant Joshi – none of whom are in the field of Model Risk- provided valuable feedback to make this book readable and understandable to individuals who are new to this exciting area.

Thanks also to Meera Joshi, my niece, who used her creative mind to design the book cover.

Finally, I'd like to thank my parents, Avinash and Mandakini Joshi, who insulated me from all the household chores while I focused on this manuscript, my other daughter, Anjali Majumdar, and my dog, Leo, who provided me with necessary distractions.

References

Board of Governors of the Federal Reserve System. "Supervisory Guidance on Model Risk Management." Supervision and Regulation Letter SR 11-7, April 4, 2011

Board of Governors of the Federal Reserve System. "Supervisory Guidance on Stress Testing for Banking Organizations with More Than $10 Billion in Total Consolidated Assets" Supervision and Regulation Letter SR 12-7, May 14, 2012

Brown, Jeffrey et. al., "Model Risk and the Great Financial Crisis: The Rise of Modern Model Risk Management", Oliver Wyman, 7 January 2015

Lopez, Linette, "How The London Whale Debacle Is Partly The Result Of An Error Using Excel", http://www.businessinsider.com/excel-partly-to-blame-for-trading-loss-2013-2, February 12, 2013

Mankotia, Sanjeev and Joshi, Aruna, "Measuring Model Risk – A Practitioner's Approach", RMA Journal Article. July/August 2013 Issue

Office of the Comptroller of the Currency. "Sound Practices for Model Risk Management: Supervisory Guidance on Model Risk Management." OCC Bulletin 2011-12, April 4, 2011

Office of the Comptroller of the Currency. "Model Validation" OCC Bulletin 2000-16, May 30, 2000

Yang, Stephanie, "The Epic Story Of How A 'Genius' Hedge Fund Almost Caused A Global Financial Meltdown", http://www.businessinsider.com/the-fall-of-long-term-capital-management-2014-7, June 10, 2014

Note from the Author

Thank you for reading this book. I hope I provided an overview of what is involved in establishing and maintaining a state of the art Model Risk Management program at a financial institution. I would love to hear from you. You can find me on LinkedIn.

Best,
Aruna Joshi

Glossary

arbitrage	simultaneous purchase and sale of an asset to profit from a difference in the price
back-test	tracking a model's output over past time and comparing it to observed values
benchmark	evaluate or check (something) by comparison with a standard
Comprehensive Capital Analysis and Review (CCAR)	a United States regulatory framework introduced by the Federal Reserve in order to assess, regulate, and supervise large banks and financial institutions
exposure	size of the portfolio of assets or liabilities
Great Recession	a term that represents the sharp decline in economic activity during the late 2000s, which is generally considered the largest downturn since the Great Depression
hedge	an investment to reduce the risk of adverse price movements in an asset
leverage	use of borrowed capital for (an investment), expecting the profits made to be greater than the interest payable
Loan loss reserves, provision	an expense set aside as an allowance for uncollected loans and loan payments. This provision is used to cover a number of factors associated with potential

	loan losses including bad loans, customer defaults and renegotiated terms of a loan that incur lower than previously estimated payments
logistic regression	a statistical method for analyzing a dataset in which there are one or more independent variables that determine an outcome. The outcome is measured with a dichotomous variable (in which there are only two possible outcomes)
macroeconomic factors	events or situations that affect the economy on a broader level, influencing the economic outcome of large groups of people on a national or regional level. Some macroeconomic factors include unemployment, savings, inflation and investments
mitigant	a factor that mitigates or alleviates something
model inventory	a central repository maintained by the model risk management group that contains all relevant aspects of model lifecycle
point-in-time	point-in-time models use macro-economic factors as opposed to through-the-cycle
quant	an expert at analyzing and managing quantitative data
risk appetite	the amount and type of risk that an organization is willing to take in order to meet its strategic objectives

scorecard	a custom model to estimate a score similar to FICO® score that usually takes the borrower aspects as well as loan aspects such as loan-to-value, loan amount etc.
SR 11-7	regulatory guidance that provides banks with a comprehensive framework for deploying an enterprise-wide model risk management program. Examiners now expect banks to use such a framework when designing, implementing and improving all models
template	a file that serves as a starting point for a new document. It is pre-formatted in some way
through-the-cycle	do not depend on any macroeconomic factors as opposed to point-in-time that do use
volatility	Rapid change and uncertainty; defined as the degree of variation of a trading price series over time as measured by the standard deviation of logarithmic returns

About the Author

Aruna Joshi has been in the quantitative finance field for over two decades spanning financial software, mortgage insurance and banking. She has a Ph.D. and MFE (Master's in Financial Engineering) from UC Berkeley. She also holds the FRM (Financial Risk Manager) Designation. She has authored several papers in top journals and is a frequent speaker at conferences related to Model Risk. She is also an adjunct faculty at University of San Francisco.

She lives in Menlo Park with her husband and has two adult daughters.

Made in United States
Troutdale, OR
05/05/2024